J G GOODE

Conspiracy And Power

Unveiling the Hidden World of Elite Families, Secret Societies, & Their Influence on Global Affairs

First edition

This book was professionally typeset on Reedsy.
Find out more at reedsy.com

Contents

Introduction

In recent years, the gap between the world's wealthiest people and the rest of the population has become impossible to ignore. As Oxfam reported in 2023 and 2025:

"The richest 1% bagged nearly twice as much wealth as the rest of the world put together over the past two years."

"Billionaire wealth surged by $2 trillion in 2024—equivalent to $5.7 billion per day—as global inequality hit unprecedented levels."

These figures raise some serious questions about the power structures that shape our world. How is it that a small group of elites control such vast amounts of wealth, while so many people struggle to meet basic needs?

Did you pick up this book because you're questioning the way power works and wondering if it's really in your best interest? Are you starting to wonder if the people who should have our well-being at heart actually do, or if powerful forces are pulling the strings behind the scenes for their own benefit?

As inequality continues to reach new extremes, it's more important than ever to take a critical look at the systems that drive global power— political, economic, and social—and to ask who really holds the power to shape our world. This concentration of wealth doesn't just divide us, it also forces us to confront how these systems are built to maintain these imbalances.

When diving into controversial topics like these, it's easy for people to dismiss them as "conspiracy theories." Yes, some of these theories may sound 'out there', but sometimes they hold a kernel of truth. It's easy to shut down strange ideas or assume the world is inherently good, and that those in power are looking out for us. But I encourage you, as you go through this book, to think beyond the ideas you've been taught by society and dig deeper—don't just take things at face value. Thinking critically will become even more important as the world speeds up, feeling like we can barely keep the pace. Trust your intuition (not your ego) to guide you toward your own truth.

What is Global Power, and how do elite families and secret societies fit in?

When we think about global power, most people picture governments, big corporations, and international organisations. In the West, we often believe these institutions are there to serve humanity's best interests, and that most people within them genuinely care about the common good. However, a growing number of people believe that wealthy families and shadowy secret societies are quietly shaping global politics, economics, and culture for their own benefit, behind the scenes.

This brings us to the term "conspiracy." The Oxford Dictionary defines a conspiracy theory as "the belief that an event or phenomenon occurs due to a conspiracy between interested parties; specifically, the idea that a covert, influential group (often politically motivated and oppressive) is behind an unexplained event."

In this book, we explore the idea that elite families and secret societies may work together to control global politics, finance, and culture to push their own agenda. These groups are believed to manipulate events and work towards creating a New World Order (an alleged world government controlled by a small elite). They use their wealth and influence to shape the world's affairs. Even though many dismiss these ideas, they still spark serious conversations about the role of powerful, secretive organisations in shaping our world.

Of course, some sceptics argue that these conspiracy theories are mostly speculative and oversimplify the complexities of global affairs. They say these theories reflect biases or misunderstandings of history. While they acknowledge the presence of wealthy and powerful families, sceptics reject the idea of a coordinated, secret group controlling world events.

This book is here to explore the controversial and often complex idea that elite families and secret societies hold significant influence over global power. As you read through the material, I encourage you to keep an open mind, consider different perspectives, and think critically as you come to your own conclusions. Understanding how power works can help us make better choices and push for a world that is more transparent and fair.

Understanding Elite Families and Their Influence

Elite families often control huge amounts of wealth, built over generations through investments in industries like finance, real estate, energy, and technology. These families usually pass down key assets, building financial empires that stretch across multiple sectors.

One of the most famous banking families in European history is the Rothschild family. Mayer Amschel Rothschild (1744–1812) set up what would grow into a massive banking empire in Europe, with his five sons helping to expand it even further. He established family businesses and homes in major cities like Vienna, London, Paris, Naples, and Frankfurt.

But while the Rothschilds' rise to power is often credited to their business skills, they've long been the target of conspiracy theories. A key example is the family's so-called "lucky break" during the Battle of Waterloo.

Thanks to their vast fortune, they had a network of agents across Europe, and Nathan Rothschild reportedly learned of Napoleon's defeat well before the official announcement. He was said to have made a huge profit by acting on this inside information, though the exact amount remains unclear. According to some reports, Nathan and his brothers made up to 135 million francs from this event.

While it's true the Rothschilds made their fortune through smart business moves, the claims about insider trading and using privileged information for personal gain raise suspicions. Whether these stories are based in fact or not, they contribute to the general mistrust many people feel toward powerful figures and the institutions they control.

The Rothschilds' wealth continues to grow. As of 2025, they are still one of the wealthiest families globally, although their fortune is no longer as centralised as it once was. Originally based in banking, the Rothschild family has diversified into industries like real estate, wine, energy, and agriculture.

The Rothschilds have undeniably played a huge role in shaping global finance and politics over the years. While many credit their success to smart business moves, their rise to power has often raised questions, especially when it comes to the amount of influence they've had in secret. Their story highlights a recurring theme about elite families—how a small group of people with vast wealth can sometimes operate behind the scenes, shaping major world events in their favour, often at the expense of the public.

A more modern example of elite power is Bill Gates, co-founder of Microsoft, who has used his wealth and influence to shape industries like technology, healthcare, and philanthropy.

As of February 12, 2025, Gates is estimated to have a net worth of $107.3 billion, according to Forbes, making him the 16th wealthiest person in the world. Meanwhile, Bloomberg's Billionaires Index puts his net worth much higher at $166 billion, ranking him 7th.

In the 1990s, Gates realised that he had an obligation to give more of his wealth to charity. In 2000, he and his wife Melinda founded the Bill & Melinda Gates Foundation, initially focusing on education, health, and local communities in the Pacific Northwest. Since then, their foundation has expanded its work, investing in low-income communities worldwide, promoting gender equality, and tackling global health issues like disease prevention and education.

Despite his philanthropy, Bill Gates is frequently the subject of conspiracy theories, particularly concerning the COVID-19 pandemic. Some claim that Gates either created the virus or orchestrated the global crisis, using vaccines as a tool for population control or to harm people. Another theory suggests that Gates is pushing for a new world order, using his influence to track and control people through technology like digital IDs and biometric data.

It's important to recognise that many of these conspiracy theories have been largely disproved by experts, including scientists, health professionals, and fact-checkers. Gates has repeatedly stated that his foundation's work is focused on improving global health, reducing poverty, and improving access to vaccines.

Nevertheless, Gates' massive wealth and influence make him a frequent target for conspiracy theorists. While his philanthropic efforts are generally aimed at helping the world's most vulnerable, they also raise questions about the amount of power one individual can have over global health policies, especially when they are tied to major government decisions worldwide. Critics argue that wealthy figures like Gates may leverage their financial power to influence public policy in ways that serve their own interests.

The Gates family's wealth and philanthropic work have certainly made a mark on global health, technology, and development. But their influence has sparked some controversy, particularly with conspiracy theories about their role in global population control and the COVID-19 pandemic. While these theories have largely been proven false, they persist, fuelled by Gates' enormous wealth, his political connections, and his involvement in global policymaking. This only adds to the larger debate about the power and influence of ultra-wealthy families, and the role they play in shaping world events and public policy.

Understanding Secret Societies and their Influence

Secret societies are groups formed around shared beliefs, values, or goals, and they tend to operate with a focus on privacy and exclusivity. These societies often have private rituals, special symbols, and hidden meetings. The idea is to foster a sense of camaraderie among members, provide support, and work toward cultural, social, or charitable objectives. Their activities can range from personal development to pushing for certain ideals or causes.

One of the most well-known and oldest fraternal organisations in the world is the Freemasons. The group's main goals are promoting mutual respect, helping members grow, and doing community service. The Freemasons trace their origins back to medieval stonemason guilds in Europe, which built massive structures like cathedrals. Over time, these guilds evolved into the Freemasonry we know today, officially taking shape in the early 18th century, especially after the first Grand Lodge was founded in London in 1717.

Freemasonry is often associated with recognisable rituals and symbols, like the Square and Compasses, the All-Seeing Eye, and the Letter G (which could stand for God, Geometry, or both). These symbols along with the secretive nature of their meetings, have led to all sorts of conspiracy theories. One of the most popular ideas is that the Freemasons secretly control global events, financial systems, and governments to push forward a "New World Order." The idea that they're behind everything is fuelled by the fact that many influential people, including U.S. Presidents, have been members. Some even claim that the Freemasons helped shape Western democracies, including influencing the drafting of the U.S. Constitution.

While the Freemasons have been tied to moral teachings and fraternal work, another secretive group that has made a significant impact in history for their focus on social reform and Enlightenment principles is The Illuminati.

The Illuminati, founded in 1776 by Adam Weishaupt in Bavaria, was all about promoting Enlightenment ideals like reason, secularism, and civil liberties. Though the Bavarian government shut it down by the late 18th century, the term "Illuminati" has become a catch-all for ideas about powerful, secretive elites controlling the world. Conspiracy theories suggest that the Illuminati still exists today, influencing politicians, financial systems, and the media in their quest to create a "New World Order."

Even though the Illuminati was officially dissolved long ago, it remains a central figure in conspiracy culture, especially in movies and media. The group's use of symbols and secret rituals only adds to its mystique, making it the symbol of hidden power and control.

The Bilderberg Group, founded in 1954, is not a secret society in the traditional sense but operates as a private conference where influential figures from politics, business, and finance gather to discuss global issues. The secrecy of their meetings, coupled with the high-profile attendees—including world leaders and top CEOs—has fuelled conspiracy theories about the group's role in shaping global policy. Critics argue that the Bilderberg Group's exclusivity allows powerful networks to advance a "New World Order" agenda, though the true extent of its influence remains speculative.

While groups like the Freemasons, Illuminati, and Bilderberg Group have certainly played big roles in shaping history and politics, how much power they really have is still up for debate. Their secrecy, powerful memberships, and use of symbolic rituals continue to stir up speculation about what they're focused on behind closed doors. Whether they're involved in charity, politics, or business, these groups highlight bigger concerns about elite power and the concentration of influence among a small, tightly-knit group of people. The appeal of secret societies isn't just about their mystery, but also about the larger questions they raise regarding transparency, power, and who's really making the decisions in global events.

The one-dollar bill features the "Eye of Providence," which symbolizes divine guidance and protection to some, while to others, it represents the "watchful eye" of surveillance and control by secret societies and elites over the masses.

Conspiracy Theories: How Elite Families and Secret Societies Operate

If, as conspiracy theorists suggest, elite families and secret societies do influence global power, how would they go about it? Let's explore some of the ways they might use their influence:

1. Controlling Financial Institutions - Many people believe that elite families and secret societies have a huge say in how central banks, major financial institutions, and big multinational companies operate. By owning big shares or having key positions, they can:

- **Direct the flow of money:** When they exert control over major investments, they can influence the success of certain industries while others face difficulties. They have the ability to dictate the flow of capital, determining the sectors that prosper and those that falter within the economy.
- **Influence monetary policy**: If they have ties to central banks (think the Federal Reserve or the European Central Bank), they can shape important decisions like interest rates, inflation, and currency values. This can lead to economic shifts such as recessions or financial crises, from which they may stand to benefit.
-

The 2008 financial crisis sparked a lot of questions about how much influence te financial elite had on the economy. It revealed major flaws in the financial system, particularly the risky behaviour of large banks and investment firms. Many of these institutions, heavily involved in subprime mortgages and complex derivatives, collapsed, causing widespread economic damage.

A key issue was how decisions by financial elites, who held influence in both business and government, led to the crisis. Governments, especially in the U.S., bailed out major banks with taxpayer money, but those responsible for the crisis faced little accountability. The crisis also highlighted how global institutions like the U.S. Treasury and the IMF often prioritise the interests of the wealthy over the public. While the rich were bailed out, millions of everyday people lost jobs and homes.

Additionally, the crisis sparked debates about the lack of financial oversight and the revolving door between Wall Street and political leaders. It raised concerns about whether public interests were being overshadowed by the influence of financial elites.

Ultimately, the crisis exposed the fragility of the economic system and the need for reforms to ensure policies benefit everyone, not just the powerful few.

2. Monopolising Key Industries - Elite families are also thought to control huge global industries like oil, finance, telecommunications, and pharmaceuticals. When they dominate these sectors, they can:

· **Control prices**: By owning key suppliers, they can impact the cost of things such as fuel or everyday products by controlling the global supply chain.

- **Influence global politics**: When they control natural resources or critical infrastructure, they can shape big decisions like wars, trade deals, and international agreements.

The Rockefeller family had a significant impact on U.S. politics through their control of the oil industry. By using their wealth and influence, they helped shape policies that favoured oil companies, including securing tax breaks and favourable regulations. This not only allowed them to dominate the industry but also helped them grow their wealth even further, solidifying their power in both business and politics.

3. Leveraging Wealth for Political Influence - Money often equals power. Elite families use their wealth to:

- **Support political movements:** By donating to political campaigns or creating political action committees (PACs), they can push through policies that suit their goals.
- **Lobbying:** Big families often lobby lawmakers to get the laws passed that align with their business interests.
- **Change leadership**: Some conspiracy theorists say these families fund revolutions or coups to make sure the new government will adopt policies that benefit their wealth.

The Koch family uses their vast wealth from Koch Industries to influence U.S. politics through political donations, lobbying, and funding think tanks and advocacy groups. These efforts help push their political agenda, particularly favouring policies that support their business interests and reduce regulations.

4. Creating Economic Crises - Some theories suggest that secret societies or powerful families could create financial crises or manipulate markets to set up situations where they can benefit. These crises can:

- **Amass wealth:** Economic recessions typically result in the failure of smaller businesses, enabling large corporations or affluent individuals to acquire assets at significantly reduced prices. This process of consolidating resources serves to increase their influence and control.

- **Bring about a "New World Order":** Some believe that major economic events, like the Great Depression or the 2008 crash, were deliberately engineered to push through global control and centralise power. In times of economic turmoil, people are more likely to accept policies that consolidate authority, such as global financial regulations or central banking systems, which benefit the powerful few.

5. Manipulating Global Trade and Markets - These families might also influence global trade by:

- **Shaping trade deals:** By getting involved in trade agreements, they can ensure the conditions are right for their industries to dominate worldwide.
- **Manipulating currencies:** They could also play with currency values to cause market instability, setting themselves up to profit when things fluctuate.

6. Philanthropy as a Tool for Influence - Philanthropy might seem like a selfless act but some argue it's a way for elite families to push their agenda:

- **Influence public policy:** By funding research or supporting charities, these families can shape policies and even education systems to align with their goals.
- **Control governments:** With their massive foundations, they can influence big organisations like the U.N. or the World Health Organisation, pushing their ideas onto global agendas.

As we talked about earlier, the Bill and Melinda Gates Foundation is a prime example of how philanthropy can wield influence.

7. Control of the Media – If powerful families and secret societies control the media, they can shape public opinion and influence decision-making. They do this by:

- **Owning the news:** By controlling multiple media outlets, they can decide what gets reported, how it gets reported, and what people believe about important events.
- **Advertising:** Having a grip on the media means they can dictate which products and services get promoted, which, in turn, affects consumer behaviour and boosts the financial power of their aligned industries.
-

The Murdoch family, owners of News Corp, controls some of the largest media outlets in the world, including Fox News and The Times. Through these outlets, they have shaped political and cultural narratives. By influencing the news content, they can sway public opinion, push specific political agendas, and impact key issues, especially in the U.S. and U.K.

8. Phasing Out Traditional Power Structures - Some conspiracy theories claim that these families are working to dismantle traditional forms of government and replace them with a more centralised global system under their control. This could mean:

- **Pushing for a global digital currency:** By pushing for cashless societies and global digital currencies, they could gain more control over economic systems. Digital currencies, managed by central banks, would centralize financial power, allowing easier monitoring and manipulation of money flows worldwide.
- **Supporting international organisations:** Groups like the WTO or the IMF might be leveraged to bypass national governments and push policies that benefit the global elite.

9. Dynastic Power - Through careful planning and strategic alliances, some dynastic families make sure their influence lasts for generations, creating a cycle of power that lasts across borders.

The Windsor family (the British royal family) is an example of this. Their royal bloodline and strategic marriages have allowed them to maintain significant influence, not just in the U.K. but on the global political stage too, especially when it comes to diplomacy and military alliances.

The Role of Media in Shaping Global Narratives

The media is a powerful tool when it comes to shaping how we see the world, and it does this in a lot of ways—sometimes by exaggerating stories, picking and choosing what to report, and spreading content that goes viral. This power directly affects how we think about subjects like power, control, and authority.

Social media platforms like Twitter, Facebook, and YouTube have become big places for conspiracy theories to spread fast. They make it easy for users to share, re-share, and amplify ideas—even if those ideas haven't been verified—and reach huge audiences. Viral posts, memes, and videos can perpetuate very quickly, and people with big followings can unintentionally, or even purposely, add credibility to these theories—even when they're not based on facts.

Social media algorithms exacerbate this by showing people more of what they already like or agree with. This can trap people in "echo chambers," where the same conspiracy theories are repeated consistently, and opposing views are rarely seen. For example, groups like "QAnon" and "anti-vaccine" movements grow strong on these platforms, with their messages spreading unchecked. The lack of real regulation on social media makes it harder to stop the spread of misinformation, and it becomes difficult for people to distinguish between fact and fiction.

While mainstream media gets significant criticism for being controlled by wealthy elites and big corporations, social media has created a space for different voices and alternative stories. Many people, frustrated with traditional news sources, turn to social media, believing they can get a wider range of viewpoints, including ones that challenge the mainstream narrative. This has fostered valuable discussions that may have previously been suppressed, but it has also facilitated the rapid spread of misinformation.

One of the most pressing challenges that arise from media's influence is the rise of "fake news" and the difficulty in discerning fact from fiction. As sensational headlines or emotionally charged content go viral, it often outpaces the fact-checking process, leading to widespread misinformation. This issue is exacerbated by the ease of sharing content without any consideration of its accuracy. Social media platforms, where posts are frequently shared without context, make it easier for misleading information to spread quickly and widely. In some cases, this misinformation is not just misleading but actively dangerous, influencing public opinion on critical issues like health, politics, and climate change.

The media's role extends beyond the spread of conspiracy theories; it also shapes how these theories are framed and discussed. When mainstream media outlets report on such theories—often in ways that sensationalise or dramatise them—they inadvertently lend them legitimacy. This, in turn, can fuel the narrative that these ideas are being suppressed by the establishment, further strengthening belief in them.

While social media provides an outlet for marginalised voices and alternative viewpoints, it also becomes a breeding ground for extremism, radicalisation, and misinformation. The viral nature of content, combined with the algorithms prioritising engagement over accuracy, can make individuals more entrenched in their beliefs, often without being exposed to opposing arguments. As a result, society faces a growing divide—not just ideologically, but in the way information is consumed and interpreted.

Ultimately, while social media opens up a whole new way for people to participate in global conversations, we have to recognise that it can both inform and mislead us. It's crucial for people to approach what they see online with a critical eye and for social media platforms to step up and take more responsibility in stopping the spread of false information.

Awakening to a new perspective on Global power

As global events unfold, public consciousness is shifting, with more people questioning traditional power structures. This shift is evident in several evolving trends:

- **Rising awareness of inequality:** People are increasingly aware of the growing divide between the wealthy and the rest of the population, prompting questions about the role elite families and secret societies might play in perpetuating this disparity.

- **Demand for transparency:** There's a growing push for more transparency, as people are increasingly sceptical about how financial and political elites are pulling the strings behind the scenes. People are starting to speak out more about how these powerful groups make decisions that benefit themselves, often at the cost to the public.

- **Impact of social media:** Platforms like Twitter, Facebook, and

YouTube are giving people more access to alternative viewpoints that mainstream media might overlook. While conspiracy theories can spread here too, they also show how much distrust people have in traditional institutions, especially those controlled by elites.

· **Activism against elite structures:** Movements like Extinction Rebellion, Black Lives Matter, and various environmental campaigns are challenging the old power structures, calling for major reforms and exposing how decisions are often controlled by powerful, unelected groups.

· **Decentralised power models:** With new technologies like blockchain and cryptocurrency, people are challenging traditional financial institutions that are tied to elite interests. These tools give individuals more control over their wealth and personal data.

· **Decreasing public confidence in governments:** As people become more aware of how powerful families and secret groups shape political decisions, trust in governments is dropping. Many feel that the needs of everyday people are being pushed aside in favour of corporate and elite interests.

· **Concerns over global governance:** As multinational corporations get bigger, more people are worried about how national sovereignty is being eroded, with global governance systems popping up that prioritise corporate interests over the needs of people. Organisations like the WTO and IMF are often criticised for helping out a small group of elites at the expense of the general public.

· **Interest in secret societies:** Groups like the Freemasons, Illuminati, and Bilderberg Group are getting more attention, as people start to question how much influence these organisations have had on global politics and history. Some see them as keeping the status quo in place, while others think they're key to understanding how power has evolved.

· **The power of digital platforms:** The internet has made it easier for people to research and share information that challenges mainstream stories. Social media and citizen journalism offer a variety of views on global power, often shedding light on things that traditional media misses.

· **Conscious consumerism:** As consumers get more aware, there's a push for companies to do more than just chase profit. People are becoming more sceptical of businesses that prioritise elite interests and are looking to support companies that focus on social impact.

- **Debate over global versus local decision-making:** With multinational corporations and secret organisations getting more powerful, there's a lot of debate over whether global elites are bypassing national governments. Many argue this undermines democracy and are calling for more regulation of powerful global networks.

In summary, the way people are starting to think about elite families and secret societies reflects a deeper understanding of how global power works. While many are still sceptical of elite influence, the rise of grassroots movements, digital platforms, and more accessible information is helping people take a more critical look at how power is spread around the world. As change happens more quickly, this shift in awareness is likely to keep influencing how we view the role of powerful networks in shaping the future.

Conclusion

To sum up, the conversation about the influence of elite families and secret societies on global power is complicated, with strong opinions on both sides. Conspiracy theorists believe these powerful groups use their wealth, connections, and influence to manipulate systems like the economy, politics, and culture for their own benefit, often from behind the scenes. They point to examples like the Rothschild family's role in banking or supposed ties between these families and global organisations as evidence of this hidden control.

On the other hand, sceptics argue that these claims are mostly speculative and oversimplify how global affairs work. While it's true that elite families have significant wealth and power, they argue that the idea of these families secretly running the world through hidden societies is a stretch. They emphasise that world events are influenced by many factors, including geopolitics, economics, and social movements—not just a small group of wealthy individuals.

Whether you believe these theories or not, it's clear that wealth plays a huge role in shaping global power, often through complex, behind-thescenes networks.

Being aware of how elite families and secret societies might influence things gives us a chance to take a closer look at global power dynamics. Questioning the stories we're told and seeking out the truths that are sometimes overlooked can help us move toward a world where those in power are more transparent, accountable, and fair.

Use this book as a jumping-off point for your own research. It's important to evaluate the evidence carefully, check your sources, and keep an open mind. Taking a balanced approach helps us better understand the complexities of global governance and the many factors that shape our world.

If you found this book engaging, I would be very appreciative if you left a favourable review of the book on Amazon.

Printed in Great Britain
by Amazon

58655096R00020